REBEL GIRLS
COURAGEOUS CANADIANS

25 TALES OF TRAILBLAZING WOMEN

Copyright © 2024 by Rebel Girls, Inc.

Rebel Girls supports copyright. Copyright fuels creativity, encourages diverse voices, promotes free speech, and creates a vibrant culture. Thank you for buying an authorized edition of this book and for complying with copyright laws by not reproducing, scanning, or distributing any part of it in any form without permission. You are supporting indie creators as well as allowing Rebel Girls to publish books for Rebel Girls wherever they may be.

Good Night Stories for Rebel Girls and Rebel Girls are registered trademarks.
Good Night Stories for Rebel Girls and all other Rebel Girls titles are available for bulk purchase for sale promotions, premiums, fundraising, and educational needs.
For details, write to sales@rebelgirls.com.

www.rebelgirls.com

This is a work of creative non-fiction. It is a collection of heartwarming and thought-provoking stories inspired by the lives and adventures of 28 influential women. It is not an encyclopedic account of the events and accomplishments of their lives.

Some of the artwork in this book has been previously published in the books *Good Night Stories for Rebel Girls, Good Night Stories for Rebel Girls: 100 Immigrant Women Who Changed the World, Good Night Stories for Rebel Girls: 100 Real-Life Tales of Black Girl Magic, Good Night Stories for Rebel Girls: 100 Inspiring Young Changemakers, Rebel Girls Animal Allies, Rebel Girls Climate Warriors, Rebel Girls Celebrate Pride, Rebel Girls Celebrate Neurodiversity, Rebel Girls Powerful Pairs, Rebel Girls Champions, Rebel Girls Level Up,* and *Rebel Girls Rock.*

Rebel Girls, Inc.
421 Elm Ave.
Larkspur, CA 94939

Created by Francesca Cavallo and Elena Favilli
Additional text by Abby Sher, Alexis Stratton, Andrea Debbink, Corinne Purtill, Margeaux Weston, Megan Clendenan, Nana Brew-Hammond, Jenelle Swan, Jestine Ware, Lilly Workneh, Sam Guss, Sarah Glenn Marsh, Sarah Parvis, Shadae Mallory, Shannon Jade, Shelbi Polk, Susan Hughes
Art direction by Giulia Flamini
Cover illustration by Salini Perera
Graphic design by Kristen Brittain
Edited by Eliza Kirby
Special thanks: Hannah Bennett, Sarah Parvis, Michon Vanderpoel, Amy Pfister, Angelique Ahlström, Andini Makosinski

Printed in China, 2023
10 9 8 7 6 5 4 3 2 1
001-342758-Mar/24
ISBN: 979-8-88964-128-5

CONTENTS

FOREWORD BY ANGELIQUE AHLSTRÖM	4
ANDINI MAKOSINSKI • Inventor	6
ANDREA BANG • Actor	8
ANGELA JAMES • Ice Hockey Player	10
ANITA SARKEESIAN • Journalist and Media Critic	12
AUTUMN PELTIER • Clean Water Activist	14
BIRUTÉ GALDIKAS • Primatologist	16
BRIGETTE LACQUETTE • Ice Hockey Player	18
BUFFY SAINTE-MARIE • Singer and Activist	20
CELINE DION • Singer	22
FRIDA VIGIL AND KATHERINE MONCADA • Activists	24
IRENE UCHIDA • Geneticist	26
JILLIAN GALLAYS • Wrestler	28
KAYUULA NOVALINGA AND SHINA NOVALINGA • Throat Singers	30
LEYLAH FERNANDEZ • Tennis Player	32
MARGARET ATWOOD • Author	34
POKIMANE • Streamer	36
PUISAND LAI • Wheelchair Basketball Player	38
QUINN • Soccer Player	40
RIYA KARUMANCHI • Inventor and Entrepreneur	42
ROSALIE ABELLA • Judge	44
SARA MAZROUEI • Planetary Geologist	46
SIYAMIYATELIYOT ELIZABETH PHILLIPS • Language Preservation Advocate	48
TANIA HALIK AND MARTINA HALIK • Cross-Country Skiers	50
VIOLA DESMOND • Entrepreneur and Activist	52
WONDAGURL • Music Producer	54
WRITE YOUR STORY	56
DRAW YOUR PORTRAIT	57
KEEP EXPLORING!	58
THE ILLUSTRATORS	62
MORE BOOKS!	63
ABOUT REBEL GIRLS	64

FOREWORD

As a child, I was fortunate to call the Canadian temperate rainforest my home. My days were filled with adventures exploring the wonders of nature, making friends with frogs, and scaling trees. My parents were avid travelers with diverse backgrounds. Together, we embarked on journeys through the rugged mountains and rivers of Colombia, took part in sweat lodge ceremonies here in Canada, and ventured into the remote corners of the wilderness for nights filled with stargazing and storytelling.

During my time at university, I found my passion in studying the incredible journey of human evolution. As I delved deeper into the records of history, I couldn't ignore the many injustices that humans and the environment had experienced. This awareness ignited within me a sense of personal responsibility toward shaping a better future. After completing a master's degree in political science and a graduate certificate in commercial space studies, I cofounded a company named Flash Forest with Bryce Jones and his brother Cameron.

As the astronomer Carl Sagan emphasized, our Earth stands alone as the only known home to life. Yet today we find our planet losing its precious forests at an unprecedented rate. That's why we started Flash Forest, a company that automates drones, using AI and plant science, to plant one billion trees, with the hope that we can rapidly restore ecosystems lost to wildfires. As the company continues to grow, I've also taken on a new endeavor to promote the well-being of our planet and its inhabitants. I recently joined the Canadian Space Agency, where I'm dedicated to shaping policies that foster a peaceful and sustainable transition into the next chapter of our story.

There are no fixed rules, predefined roadmaps, or limits dictating how you can make an impact during your time on Earth. The struggles our planet faces today call for more perspectives, skills, and talents than ever before. We need inspiring leadership from inventors, singers, astronauts, policymakers, entrepreneurs, and writers. In all these fields, imagination and inspiration are our strongest tools to shape a brighter world.

And it's precisely this celebration of imagination and inspiration that makes Rebel Girls so important. *Rebel Girls: Courageous Canadians* takes us on a journey to Canada. You'll read about the great writer Margaret Atwood, Indigenous language-preservation activist Siyamiyateliyot Elizabeth Phillips, and a wealth of others paving the way in clean water activism, primatology, planetary geology, sports, music, genetics, and more. Their contributions have addressed some of our world's most critical challenges. In this book, you will learn about the obstacles these Canadian women overcame, demonstrating how our potential is truly untapped.

Our imagination knows no bounds. Changing the world may seem like a daunting, lonely journey, but it's anything but that. Moments of doubt can serve as the spark that propels us to reshape our approach to life. These sparks inspire us to become the very best versions of ourselves while extending our focus beyond our own lives, considering how we can best serve our world, not just for ourselves but for future generations. To me, this is one of the important messages that permeate the powerful stories of the Canadian women featured in this book. To chart new paths in the face of doubt, we can find inventive ways to dare to do what hasn't been done.

More than ever, we need Rebel Girls—like you.

—Angelique Ahlström

BONUS! AUDIO STORIES!

Download the Rebel Girls app to hear longer stories about some of the impactful creators and leaders in this book and discover tales of other trailblazing women. When you come across a QR code in this book, scan it, and you'll be whisked away on an audio adventure.

SCAN TO HEAR MORE!

ANDINI MAKOSINSKI

INVENTOR

SCAN TO HEAR MORE!

Once upon a time, a girl named Andini visited a friend's home that didn't have electricity. It was too dark for them to study!

Andini was great at building things, and she was especially passionate about transistors, devices that regulate the flow of electric current.

"What if I could invent a flashlight that is powered by your body?" Andini asked her friend. "After all, our bodies give off lots of energy in the form of heat." The girls got very excited.

"Just think how many people could have electricity if this worked!"

Andini was just 15 years old, but she already had a lot of experience taking things apart and putting them back together.

So she started to work on this mysterious new flashlight. She called it the "Hollow Flashlight" because she built it using a hollow aluminum tube that cooled the heat collected from the holder's hand.

When she presented it to the Google Science Fair, she won first prize! It's the first flashlight that doesn't need batteries, wind, or sun—just body heat.

Today Andini is considered one of the most promising inventors of our time. Her dream is to make the battery-free Hollow Flashlights available to anyone in the world who can't afford electricity.

"I like the idea of using technology to make the world a better place and to keep our environment clean," she always says.

BORN OCTOBER 3, 1997

ANDREA BANG

ACTOR

Andrea had many ideas about what she wanted to do when she grew up. Maybe she'd be a librarian, a construction worker, or a cashier. Maybe a fashion designer, a graphic designer, or a fairy. Maybe . . . an actor?

No. That's impossible, thought Andrea. Not one of the actors she saw on television looked like her, a Korean Canadian girl.

Plus, her parents wanted her to get a reliable job with a steady income. They had immigrated to Canada from Seoul, South Korea, and opened a laundromat outside Vancouver. They dreamed of a stress-free life for Andrea. Acting sounded way too unstable to them.

So Andrea tried to put her acting dream away and headed off to university to study psychology. But soon she volunteered as a production assistant on a movie her classmate was making. Then she wrote her own short film and acted in it, and before long she was acting in other student films.

It was impossible, but . . .

Andrea kept acting. A few years later, she had an opportunity to audition for a role on a new comedy TV show. Should she reach for her impossible dream?

She did—and she got the part!

Kim's Convenience was the first Canadian show with an Asian-led cast. It was about a Korean Canadian family's adventures running a convenience store. Andrea played Janet Kim, the strong-willed daughter who studied art and cared deeply about her parents and brother, even when they were at odds. Audiences loved the show's humor and heart—and especially how real the Kim family felt.

"When I was growing up, I didn't have a show like this to watch," Andrea said. Now she is a role model for other Asian Canadian kids chasing what seem like impossible dreams.

BORN MAY 2

ANGELA JAMES

ICE HOCKEY PLAYER

Once upon a time, there was a girl who was sweet and nice but vicious on the ice! Her name was Angela. She grew up in a tough neighborhood in Toronto and stayed active by playing street hockey with her sisters. She loved it! She ran around with a hockey stick and slapped the black puck into the net, scoring goal after goal.

There weren't any girls' or women's ice hockey leagues near her. So her mother signed her up for the boys' league.

Angela proved to everyone that she was just as good as the boys—and better than most. She was so good, in fact, that she was holding her own on the ice with boys who were three years older than her.

Sadly, after just one year, Angela was kicked off the team. The reason was clear to Angela: the league didn't like that the best player on a boys' team was a girl!

Later, Angela joined a girls' league. She had to take a long bus ride to attend her games, but she didn't mind. She'd do anything to play! Soon the Central Ontario Women's Hockey League invited 16-year-old Angela to join a team. With her helmet and skates, she was ready to go!

Angela was a powerhouse on the ice—an unstoppable force when she headed for the goal. She played for 20 years, racking up wins and gold medals. Her record-breaking skills landed her in the Hockey Hall of Fame, where she made history as the first Black woman and the first openly gay player to be inducted.

BORN DECEMBER 22, 1964

ANITA SARKEESIAN

JOURNALIST AND MEDIA CRITIC

Anita loved video games. As a little girl growing up in Canada, she begged her parents for a Nintendo Game Boy of her own. When she was in high school, she spent hours playing on the computer. Video games were fun, and they made her happy.

But as she got older, she noticed something that bothered her. There were hardly any female game characters—and extremely few strong, positive female ones.

This wasn't the first time Anita had noticed something amiss in the media. When she was younger, Anita had seen that people from Iraq—the country her parents were from—were often portrayed on television as scary or bad. She didn't see any representations that looked like the people she loved. Anita realized that sometimes the media told stories that weren't accurate or left important things out.

Anita started her own website, a blog called *Feminist Frequency*. She posted a series of videos in which she talked to viewers about the way women were depicted in video games.

Her videos were smart and funny, and made people in the gaming industry think about how to make their products better for men and women alike. But some men who saw the videos didn't want to hear any new ideas. They called her ugly names. Some even threatened to hurt her.

Anita refused to be silent, and the more she spoke up, the more people listened. Today there are more women than ever in video games—both as characters on the screen and as engineers designing them.

BORN MAY 2, 1989

AUTUMN PELTIER

CLEAN WATER ACTIVIST

SCAN TO
HEAR MORE!

Once upon a time, there was a girl who believed that all water was sacred. Her name was Autumn, and she was born in the Wikwemikong Unceded Indian Reserve, on Manitoulin Island, Canada.

Autumn loved being silly, making slime with her sister, and texting with friends. But she was very serious about protecting the water people drink and the water that nourishes animals and plants and allows trees to grow tall.

Growing up in the Ojibwe/Odawa heritage, Autumn began performing water ceremonies when she was very little. She would walk through fierce winter winds with her elders and kneel on a frozen lake. She'd make a hole in the ice and dip in a special copper cup, scooping out water and chanting a prayer of protection.

When Autumn was eight years old, she attended a water ceremony. Signs all over read, "DON'T DRINK THE WATER." She learned that underground pipelines had contaminated the water. It broke her heart.

In 2016, Autumn was chosen to present the Canadian prime minister with a special gift at an annual gathering for the First Nations. With thousands of eyes watching, she took a deep breath and handed him a copper water bowl. Then she said, "I am very unhappy with the choices you've made."

She told him that he was hurting her people by allowing pipelines to pollute their water. The crowd was shocked and inspired, and the prime minister promised to help.

Since that day, Autumn has traveled around the world, raising her voice and demanding that leaders respect and protect our waters. As she says, "Water is everything. It's the lifeblood of Mother Earth."

BORN SEPTEMBER 27, 2004

BIRUTÉ GALDIKAS

PRIMATOLOGIST

Biruté found her favorite type of animal in the first book she ever checked out of the library: *Curious George*.

She fell in love with all monkeys and apes. Chimpanzees, bonobos, gorillas—they all captured her attention. But one type of ape stood out: orangutans. When she looked at pictures of them, Biruté saw intelligence. *Are they as curious as I am?* she wondered.

When she got older, Biruté moved to Borneo, a giant island in southeast Asia, where wild orangutans roamed. She followed the animals for years, researching and learning more about orangutans than anyone else on the planet.

All that knowledge made her the perfect person to call when an orphaned orangutan needed help. Conservation officials handed Biruté the small orange creature, and she couldn't help but laugh. This was it. She was holding a baby ape just like Curious George! The orangutan wrapped his tiny hand around her finger when she fed him from a baby bottle.

Biruté taught him how to survive in the wild. She caught him when he tumbled out of trees as he started to climb and swing. She showed him how to pick ripe fruit. She encouraged his curiosity and helped him learn how to stay safe in the jungle. It was a sad day when he was finally ready to leave her side, but Biruté was proud. And she wasn't lonely for long. Soon, there was another orphaned orangutan who needed her.

When Biruté had her own son, his playmates were fuzzy baby orangutans. In nearly 50 years of research, Biruté has sent more than 500 little apes back out to the wild where they belong.

BORN MAY 10, 1946

BRIGETTE LACQUETTE

ICE HOCKEY PLAYER

By the time Brigette was five years old, she was already on a mission. She wanted to join a hockey team. But that wasn't so easy for a little girl in the small First Nations community of Mallard, Manitoba. About four hours northwest of the city Winnipeg, Mallard had a firehouse, a water pump, and fewer than 120 people. What it didn't have was a hockey rink.

Lucky for Brigette, she had a family who saw the spark in her. They recognized her talent when she laced up her skates and chased her brothers across the ice. So her father flooded the backyard and built her a rink, right on the family lawn. And when she joined the closest team (it was still far away), her whole family pitched in to get her to practices and games.

As a child, Brigette developed eczema, an uncomfortable skin condition. When it flared up, she would itch like crazy! Some kids bullied her, making fun of her blotchy, irritated skin. But when Brigette suited up for hockey practice, her gear covered her like armor and protected her from the taunts of her classmates.

She shined on the ice! Even as a teenager, she made powerful shots and mapped out clever paths so she could zip past the opposing defense. But she wasn't always accepted. At 12 years old, playing in her first big tournament, she heard words that stung. *Go back to the reservation*, spat an opponent. Another called her a nasty name. Shocked and hurt, she looked to her father for advice. "Beat them on the ice," he said.

Brigette took her father's advice and didn't look back. She played in college and competed in the World Championships. And, in 2018, she was the first First Nations player on the Canadian women's Olympic hockey team.

BORN NOVEMBER 10, 1992

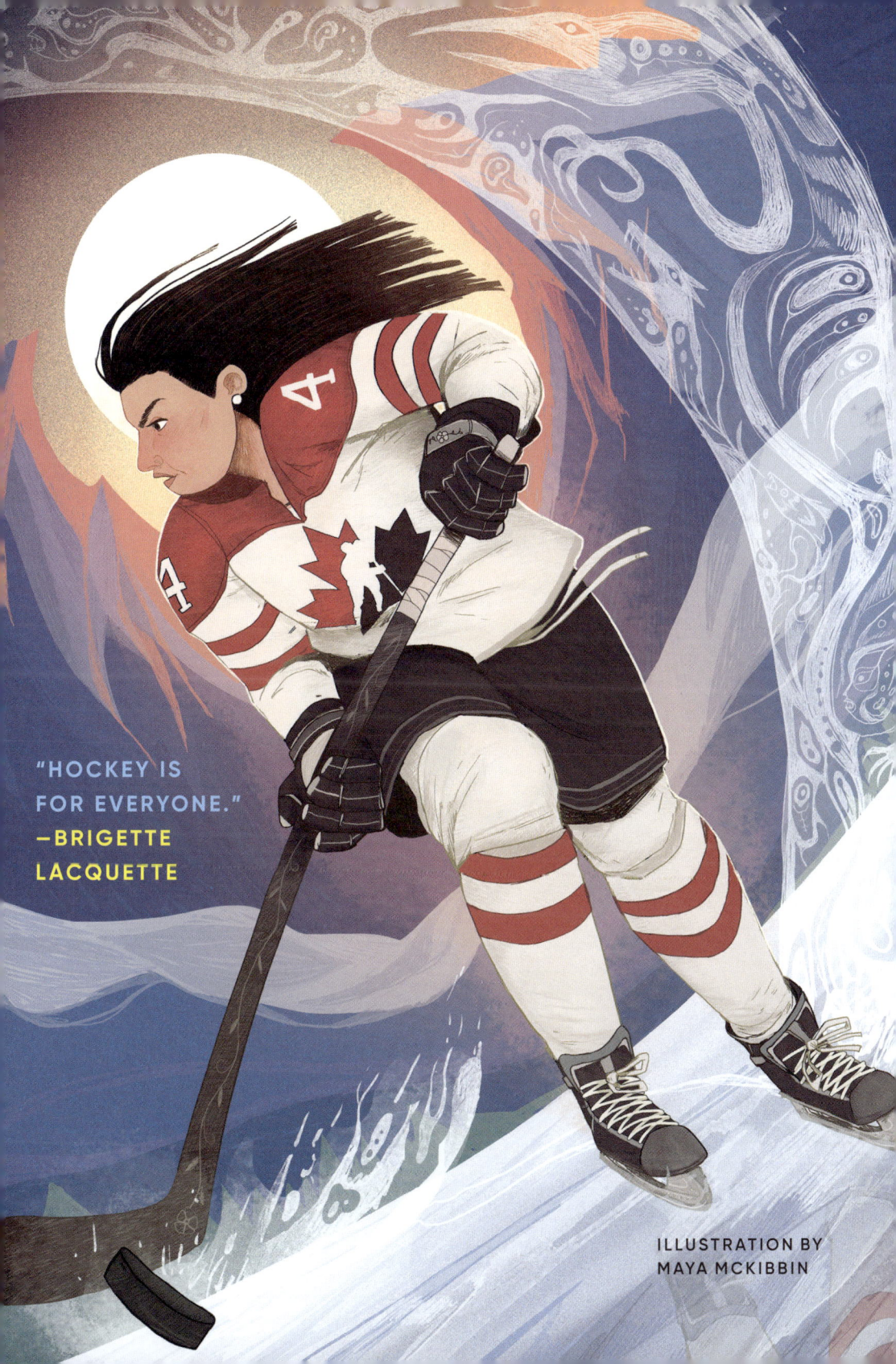

BUFFY SAINTE-MARIE

SINGER AND ACTIVIST

Once upon a time, there was a girl named Buffy who grew up filled with wonder and curiosity. At the time she was born, the government often cruelly separated Indigenous children like Buffy from their families, leaving no records of their birth. When she was an infant, Buffy was taken from her home and adopted by a couple in Maine in the United States. Her new mom was of European descent but also part Mi'kmaq. Sometimes Buffy wondered, *Who am I related to?*

As a little kid, Buffy fell in love with music. She taught herself to play guitar and piano, singing along with her rich vibrato voice. And as she grew up, she learned all she could about Indigenous cultures, went to college, and sang her songs.

One summer when she was in Canada, a friend introduced her to a family from the Piapot Cree Nation in Saskatchewan, and they became friends. Later the Piapot family adopted her in remembrance of a child they had lost many years before. The experience made Buffy want to celebrate Indigenous issues and people, and she continued to travel and learn. In her songs, she spoke out about equality, love, hope, and Indigenous rights.

Buffy also became a regular on the children's TV show *Sesame Street*. A lot of times when kids learned about Indigenous people, they learned only about the past. But Buffy wanted them to know: "We are alive and real. We have fun, friends, families."

Year after year, Buffy kept standing up for what she believed in. When she had a baby in 1976, few women in North America were breastfeeding, especially in public. So Buffy decided to be the first person to nurse a baby on national television—right on Sesame Street!

Buffy continues to be a fierce activist, singing her messages of love and hope, loud and strong.

BORN FEBRUARY 20, 1941

CELINE DION

SINGER

Once upon a time in a tiny town in Québec, a girl named Celine lived in a home bursting with brothers and sisters. Life with 13 older siblings wasn't always easy. Her family didn't have a lot of money, but they always had music. Each night, her parents played lively rhythms on the accordion and the fiddle, and everyone sang. Celine stood on the kitchen table with a fork in her hand, pretending it was a microphone. She adored those nights.

When Celine was five years old, her brother Michel asked her to sing a solo at his wedding. She was petrified. *Do all these people want to listen to me?* she wondered. At first, Celine stood frozen. Then she began to sing—and she didn't want to stop. *This is what I want to do*, she thought. *I want to be a singer!*

Celine practiced long hours, studying lyrics and learning how to breathe as she sang. When she was 12, people in the music industry began to notice her. At 13, she appeared on a television show. Beneath the bright studio lights, Celine felt stage fright creeping up inside her. The music started. Could she really do this? At last, her strong voice soared. The audience loved her!

By the time she was 14, she had released two albums. When she was 16, Celine went on tour with some famous rock bands. She was the opening act. Some nights the audience turned away or talked over her—they were there for the main event, not this unknown opener! But Celine kept singing anyway. She never gave up.

Since then, she has released many albums in both French and English, toured the world, and won international contests. Belting out the lyrics with her powerful voice, she sings about love, dreams, and courage. The little girl who sang on the kitchen table has become one of the best-selling musicians of all time.

BORN MARCH 30, 1968

FRIDA VIGIL AND KATHERINE MONCADA

ACTIVISTS

Once upon a time, there were two girls who struggled to feel like they belonged.

At five years old, Frida moved with her family from El Salvador to faraway Canada. Frida had to learn a new culture and a new language. At home, she ate comforting bowls of *sopa de frijoles*, one of the Salvadoran foods that Frida's parents continued to cook. But as the years in Canada went by, Frida lost touch with many traditions from her home country. "I feel like I turned my back on being Salvadoran," Frida said. She worried about what might happen to her culture once her parents were gone. *Who will make the sopa de frijoles?*

When she was 16, Katherine and her family moved to Canada from Nicaragua. As they adjusted to life in Canada, her family began to speak a mix of Spanish and French—it got confusing! Katherine remembered her culture, but she felt concerned about her younger siblings. *Will they forget they are Nicaraguan?*

Both Katherine and Frida wondered what other young Canadians with Latin American heritage felt about their identities. They decided to find out.

Together, they launched a campaign called #ShowUsYourLatinRoots. They prepared interview questions and short videos. Their excitement grew. When they were ready to interview people, Frida asked, microphone in hand: "What does being Latin American Canadian mean to you?"

The responses helped people—including Frida and Katherine—understand that they can embrace the beauty of many cultures. *My family can connect with both worlds!* Katherine realized. *Maybe in the future I'll make sopa de frijoles!* Frida thought. Now both Frida and Katherine know exactly where they belong.

FRIDA: BORN JUNE 5, 1997 • KATHERINE: BIRTHDATE UNKNOWN

IRENE UCHIDA

GENETICIST

It was November 1941. Irene had just arrived home in Canada from a long trip to Japan. World War II was in full swing, and Irene was able to make it out on the last boat leaving Yokohama. But when she got back, she was met with terrible news. Some people were afraid that Japanese Canadians like her might be helping the enemy in the war. So the government made the cruel decision to put thousands of ordinary citizens into internment camps, which were usually reserved for prisoners of war.

Irene, her family, and more than 20,000 other Japanese Canadians were forced to leave their homes and jobs and live in cramped, unsafe quarters. Irene's camp was filled with frightened families with young children. She began teaching the kids at the camp and took an interest in what made each one different.

After the war, Irene studied genetics—the science of the genes kids inherit from their parents. Genes control eye color, hair color, and sometimes diseases. She opened a lab to research disorders like Down syndrome, a condition where some people are born with an extra chromosome. Chromosomes are tiny building blocks inside every person that contain their genes. When someone is born with an extra one, they look and act differently than people who have the typical amount. *What if those extra chromosomes could be detected before a baby was born?* Irene wondered.

Irene worked hard to develop a test for chromosome numbers. With Irene's test, parents could learn more about their baby's genes—even before the baby was born! She also determined that radiation, like X-rays, could cause Down syndrome. These discoveries changed the way doctors care for pregnant people and their babies. Irene encouraged scientists to "find every possible way to help people."

APRIL 8, 1917–JULY 30, 2013

JILLIAN GALLAYS

WRESTLER

The wrestling mat felt soft beneath Jillian's feet. She waited for her cue to start the match. Although she was nervous, she reminded herself she didn't get the nickname Jilla Killa for nothing. Competing in the Olympics had always been a dream of Jillian's, and she was thrilled to be representing Team Canada.

When she was young, Jillian looked forward to going to school—not for the classroom but for the wrestling mat. Jillian started wrestling competitively in ninth grade. She enjoyed being on the mat. There, she felt like her true self. The other parts of school, though, weren't as fun for Jillian. Growing up, she had a hard time reading, writing, and spelling. She would mix up letters, write words backward, and even form letters upside down. It made it difficult for Jillian to learn. She didn't know why until a doctor told her she had dyslexia.

In college, Jillian worked toward a degree in kinesiology, the study of human body movement. She did well on the college wrestling team, but she struggled with her courses—they were harder than any classes she'd taken before. But she didn't give up. In order to continue wrestling, Jillian had to keep her grades up. It took seven years to finish her degree, and Jillian graduated in 2012. Then she set out to tackle her next dream: to compete in the Olympic Games.

Jillian trained with all her heart, practicing her pins, escapes, and takedowns. She won the Canadian National Champion title six times before competing in the 2016 Summer Olympics. Jillian did not win a medal, but with her determination and perseverance, she knows that more great things are in store for her.

BORN 20 OCTOBER 1986

KAYUULA NOVALINGA AND SHINA NOVALINGA

THROAT SINGERS

Kayuula and her daughter, Shina, were both born in Nunavik, Canada, which is full of snowcapped mountains, wide sparkling lakes, caribou, and polar bears. Kayuula and Shina are part of the Indigenous Inuit people, who have lived on this land for almost a thousand years. Many Inuits spend time in the wilderness, hunting and harvesting. They are known for their sewing and printmaking, and the way they tell stories through a special kind of music called throat singing.

Standing face to face, Kayuula makes a low, breathy sound. Then, Shina tries to match that sound. Kayuula adds a rhythm with her voice, and Shina does the same. They go back and forth, sometimes with high-pitched bird calls and sometimes with exhales that sound like rushing wind. Pretty soon, it's hard to tell who is leading and who is following.

Throat singing is a sacred tradition for the Inuit. In the early 1900s, colonists who wanted to take over the Inuit lands outlawed throat singing. As time moved on, fewer and fewer people practiced it. But as Shina says, "We are now taking it back and passing it down to keep it alive."

In March 2020, Shina began posting videos of their songs online. People were amazed by their voices. Shina then started sharing insights about Inuit culture and showing off the clothing that Kayuula made for her by hand.

As Shina and Kayuula become more and more popular, they've used their voices not only to sing but also to talk about Indigenous rights and raise money for Indigenous communities in need. They celebrate their past and present and urge people to help protect their future.

KAYUULA: BORN 1977 • SHINA: BORN 1998

"THE CONNECTION BETWEEN MY MOTHER AND ME GROWS BIGGER AS WE THROAT SING TOGETHER. IT'S ALWAYS A BEAUTIFUL MOMENT FOR US."
—SHINA NOVALINGA

ILLUSTRATION BY ANDRESSA MEISSNER

LEYLAH FERNANDEZ

TENNIS PLAYER

Once upon a time in the Canadian city of Montreal, there lived a small girl with a huge amount of determination. Her name was Leylah, and she loved to play tennis.

When she was five, Leylah used to stand in the driveway and hit the ball against the house or go down to the basement and hit the ball against the wall. Her mom worried she'd break the car or the TV. So Leylah and her sister would ride their bikes to the tennis courts and practice there.

A few years later, her parents enrolled her in a sports development program. But Leylah wasn't as good as the other kids. Soon, she was dropped from the program. Leylah was crushed, but she refused to quit. When her parents saw her fierce determination, her father began coaching her.

Once, Leylah's elementary school teacher told her, *Stop playing tennis. You'll never make it. Just focus on school.*

Many people thought Leylah was too small to play well. *She can't hit the ball with power!*

Leylah was upset—but once again, she wouldn't give up.

Her dad was with her every step of the way. He told Leylah they had to work hard every day. She was small, but she was fast and agile—and she had to develop those skills, darting across the court to return shots that her opponents were sure she'd miss. *There's no limit to what you can do*, he said.

Leylah agreed. She worked hard and kept improving.

And she and her father were right. By the time she was 17, Leylah was a professional tennis player, and by the time she was 19, she was ranked the 13th best women's tennis player in the world. And it's all thanks to that small girl's big determination.

BORN SEPTEMBER 6, 2002

 # MARGARET ATWOOD

AUTHOR

Once upon a time, there was a girl named Margaret who wrote poetic essays about her pet praying mantis. She was fascinated by how smart the little critter was. She even trained it to walk up her arm and drink out of a spoon!

Margaret also had a pet butterfly. For her, tiny creeping, buzzing, or flying creatures were just as vibrant a part of life as the fungi and the woodlands she loved to observe. Her father was a biologist who studied forest insects. And his work took the family through some of the wildest woods in Canada.

As she grew up, her interest in the wonders of the natural world and the role science could play in it inspired her more and more. In school, she wrote an operetta featuring a teddy bear made of wool who was sad that he shrunk every time he was washed. When he fell in love with a princess made of scientifically created fabric, he got his happy ending—a baby made of a wool blend that did not shrink in the dryer.

Margaret expanded on these themes when she became a published author. One of her most celebrated works is a three-book series about a future society suffering from a distorted relationship between nature and science. Her words got readers all over the world thinking more seriously about climate change. Margaret encourages people to consider the role they can play to protect the planet and then to take action. She wants the next generation to enjoy the enchanted harmony she experienced as a child with her pet insects and the wild mushrooms and thickets of trees in the wilderness.

BORN NOVEMBER 18, 1939

POKIMANE

STREAMER

Once upon a time, a little girl in Canada fell in love with gaming while watching her brother play *Pokémon*. Imane sat, entranced, as beautiful worlds came to life on handheld screens and TV sets. With her controller in hand, she could dash across the screen as a Pokémon trainer or battle a warlock in *The Legend of Zelda*, unraveling amazing stories that stayed with her as she grew up.

Later, Imane switched from playing pixelated adventures on her bedroom floor to exploring online games with friends. When she was done playing, she would watch other girl gamers post their gaming adventures online. *I could do that too!* she thought.

Imane created a Twitch account called "Pokimane," a combination of her name and *Pokémon*, which ignited her love of gaming. As Pokimane, she streamed videos of herself playing *Fortnite and League of Legends*.

Imane's audience started out small, and she struggled to find her place on Twitch as a girl gamer. Sometimes, it was frustrating, but the more she played, the more her audience grew. One day, as she looked at the number of viewers watching her videos, she realized she could make streaming her full-time job. Maybe she could inspire other little girls to share their favorite games, as well.

Imane has become one of the most viewed female Twitch streamers online. Millions of people all over the world watch her videos. She hopes that when other girls see her streams, they'll understand there's a place for them in gaming too.

BORN MAY 14, 1996

PUISAND LAI

WHEELCHAIR BASKETBALL PLAYER

Puisand had always dreamed of being an athlete. As a little girl, she was constantly on the move—running and racing and jumping all around.

When Puisand was six years old, she received life-changing news. She was diagnosed with a rare nerve condition. Puisand had to start using a wheelchair, and many people thought her athletic dreams were dashed. But there was no way she was quitting.

When she was 13, Puisand joined a wheelchair tennis program. She wanted to make friends and learn the game. Shocked and proud, she found out she was more talented than she'd realized. She could hit the tennis ball with a powerful whack! and race across the court faster than anyone else.

A year later, Puisand set off to a tennis camp for people using wheelchairs. She practiced her pivots, swings, and serves. By 2017, she was listed as seventh in the International Tennis Federation rankings for girls' wheelchair tennis. But was one sport enough? Not for Puisand! She set her sights on becoming an all-round sports superstar.

When Puisand started wheelchair basketball, she picked it up quickly and was soon recruited to join Team Ontario. She won gold at the 2017 Ontario Winter Games and competed at the 2018 Wheelchair Basketball World Championship as part of the Canadian national team. Then, in 2021, one of Puisand's biggest dreams came true—she competed in the Paralympic Games in Tokyo.

BORN JULY 29, 2000

QUINN

SOCCER PLAYER

What do you want to be when you grow up? Quinn's first-grade teacher asked their class.

Quinn's eyes lit up. They knew exactly what they wanted to be. They pursed their lips together as their crayon swept across their paper. Slowly, Quinn's picture became clear: a blond-haired, blue-eyed person stood on an Olympic podium wearing a shiny gold medal around their neck.

Which sport was being celebrated was anyone's guess. Quinn's parents drove them and their sisters all over Toronto—to hockey practice, ski lessons, and swim team.

But most of all, Quinn loved soccer. Quinn dribbled down the field, dodged between orange cones, and slammed the ball into the goal. They came home sweaty and exhausted. But they never gave up.

Finally, when they were 18, they made Canada's national soccer team. They were thrilled!

In 2021, Quinn and their teammates flew to Tokyo, Japan, to compete in the Olympic Games. Canada played hard every match, and they made their way to the top. Finally, in their last game, Canada beat Sweden in a high-stakes shoot-out. Quinn and their teammates rushed onto the field, cheering and hugging one another.

Not only did Canada's women's soccer team win gold for the very first time, but Quinn made history too—as the first out trans and nonbinary medalist in the Olympics. When an official placed the medal around Quinn's neck, they remembered the picture they'd drawn in first grade. They looked at their teammates, who had helped them reach this magical day, and smiled. They couldn't stop smiling if they tried.

BORN AUGUST 11, 1995

RIYA KARUMANCHI

INVENTOR AND ENTREPRENEUR

Riya was visiting a friend's house when she noticed that her friend's grandmother kept bumping into things. She had a visual impairment, and the white cane she used when she walked around hadn't been updated in a century. It was just a stick! *Don't my friend's grandmother—and all visually impaired people—deserve to benefit from advances in technology and design?* she thought.

Riya decided that it was about time someone made a smarter cane. For a school science fair project, Riya and a friend worked on a prototype of a cane with a sensor that would allow visually impaired people to "see" objects above the knee. Their SmartCane won first prize!

But for Riya, SmartCane wasn't just a project for a science fair. She kept working on it, bringing it to hackathons, where she learned to code and develop the technology in the cane further. She added new features, like a GPS that vibrated to give SmartCane users directions: one buzz for left, two buzzes for right. Riya even studied business so she could turn SmartCane into a real product, available on the market. Big tech companies were so impressed with her work and creativity that they invested tens of thousands of dollars in her business.

What was it like to be a young inventor? reporters asked Riya. "We're living in one of the best times in history to create things and pursue our passions," she replied. "And there are more resources than ever before to help you." Nothing should stop kids from working on their big ideas. "The worst that can happen is you learn," said Riya with a twinkle in her eye.

BORN CIRCA 2003

"PEOPLE MAY NOT ALWAYS LIKE YOUR IDEA, AND YOU HAVE TO WORK HARD FOR IT AND PUT IN THE EFFORT AND TIME. THAT'S WHAT WILL GET YOU PLACES."
—RIYA KARUMANCHI

ILLUSTRATION BY AVANI DWIVEDI

ROSALIE ABELLA

JUDGE

Once upon a time, there was a girl named Rosalie who knew how important it was for laws to treat everyone with the same respect. Her parents were Polish Jewish people who had survived World War II, and Rosalie was born in a displaced persons camp.

Rosalie's family moved to Canada when she was small, and although her father had been a lawyer in Germany, he was not allowed to practice law in Canada because he was not a citizen.

Only four years after Rosalie became a lawyer herself, she was asked to serve as a judge in Canada's family court. She was the first Jewish woman to become a judge in Canada and one of the youngest judges in the country's history. She was also the first person in Canada to become a judge while pregnant!

Every day she saw people struggling in a system that treated them unfairly because of their gender, disability, or skin color. Rosalie tried her best to listen with an open mind and be fair in her decisions.

"I learned to see law from the experiences of the people who were before me..." Rosalie said later. "Looking at the law and justice from their eyes taught me how to be a judge."

Around 1984, Rosalie was put in charge of a huge job: to figure out how to make workplaces in Canada more equal to all workers. Her report was used in other countries to make their workplaces fairer too.

In 2004, Rosalie became the first Jewish woman to serve on Canada's Supreme Court.

BORN JULY 1, 1946

SARA MAZROUEI

PLANETARY GEOLOGIST

Once there was a girl in Iran who wanted to blaze her own trail like a comet in the night sky. Sara spent her childhood marveling at outer space and reading books about brave girls who weren't afraid to be different. It was good training for what was to come.

When Sara was 13, her family moved to Canada so she and her sisters could study and be whatever they wanted. Things were different in Canada, but not all doors were open the way they'd hoped.

Sara dreamed of being a NASA scientist. While working on her PhD, she was chosen for a NASA internship, but a few weeks after she arrived, Sara received unexpected news: she didn't have security clearance to be at NASA because she had been born in Iran. The officials even questioned how she had gotten the internship. Sara was frustrated—she had been honest about her birthplace from the beginning.

Nevertheless, Sara's sense of adventure and her love of math and science propelled her to finish her internship, get her PhD, and become a planetary scientist. She went on to teach others about space and to study things including the history of asteroids and the best landing locations for future lunar missions. She also spoke out for equality. She believed that people should be free to be leaders in STEM careers, no matter their gender or where they're from. "I wonder how much more I could've achieved," Sara said, "if I didn't have to spend half of my time defending the fact that I belong where I am."

BORN NOVEMBER 3, 1987

SIYAMIYATELIYOT ELIZABETH PHILLIPS

LANGUAGE PRESERVATION ADVOCATE

Once there was a girl named Siyamiyateliyot who spoke a language that almost nobody else did. The language was called Upriver Halq'eméylem. She and the others in her small Indigenous community were the only ones in the world to speak it. Their nation was the Stó:lō. It was named after the Stó:lō, or Fraser River, which ran past their territory near Vancouver, BC.

When she was seven, Siyamiyateliyot was sent to live at a residential school. Many Indigenous children at the time were forced to leave their homes because the government wanted them to blend in with white Canadian culture. She was given the English name Elizabeth. She wasn't allowed to speak Halq'eméylem anymore.

But Siyamiyateliyot refused to give in. The Stó:lō ran past the school, cutting a wide blue path through the green mountains. She looked out at it and thought in her language. No one could stop her from doing that!

Years passed. Siyamiyateliyot and her classmates finally got to go home. She still remembered how to speak Halq'eméylem, but the other kids didn't.

This is a huge problem, Siyamiyateliyot realized. Halq'eméylem wasn't a written language. It only stayed alive because people spoke it. When everyone who spoke it died, her language would die too.

I must keep our language alive! Siyamiyateliyot decided. She and a group of Stó:lō Elders made sound recordings of Halq'eméylem words and created a dictionary. A researcher even took videos and ultrasounds of her lips and tongue while she spoke. This would help students learn to pronounce difficult sounds.

Today, Siyamiyateliyot is the last known fluent speaker of Halq'eméylem. And she proudly continues her work to keep her language alive.

BORN 1939

TANIA HALIK AND MARTINA HALIK

CROSS-COUNTRY SKIERS

Once upon a time, a girl named Martina and her mother, Tania, set out on an epic journey. Together, they would cross-country ski the length of Canada's Coast Mountains.

Tania dehydrated food like fruit, nuts, meat, and granola in her kitchen. The packages of food filled up the living room. They couldn't possibly carry it all! They had to have it flown by helicopter to special food drop sites. Still, they would need to carry a two-person tent, sleeping bags, a change of warm clothes, an emergency kit, a camp cook stove, glacier-climbing gear, and a blow-up raft so they could get across any rivers in their path.

After a year of planning, Martina and Tania set off from Squamish, British Columbia. Each day, they walked, skied, and climbed a sea of ice, rock, and snow. Each night, they made camp to try to warm up.

The wind whipped around their little orange tent. It shuddered and shivered as if trying to shake off snow flurries. Martina and Tania savored their hot chocolate and cuddled up in their sleeping bags for warmth.

The trip was grueling. But it was also filled with unforgettable beauty. Glittering fields stretched as far as the eye could see. Mountaintops jutted out of fluffy pillows of snow. They gazed in awe at a piercing blue ice cave that rose up around them like a frozen cathedral.

Finally, six months after their journey began, Martina and Tania emerged from the forest. They arrived in Skagway, Alaska, on a rainy, cold day in early spring. With huge grins, they hugged each other and cried.

Tania and Martina were the first team of women to make this journey.

TANIA: BIRTHDATE UNKNOWN • MARTINA: BIRTHDATE UNKNOWN

VIOLA DESMOND

ENTREPRENEUR AND ACTIVIST

Growing up in Nova Scotia, a province in eastern Canada, Viola noticed that ads for hair products showed only white people. She wanted to open a salon for Black women. But because she was Black, Viola could not find a local beauty school that would admit her. So she traveled to Montreal, Atlantic City, and New York City to take courses. She even trained with the legendary Madam C. J. Walker!

Later, Viola returned home and opened the city's first Black hair salon for women. But she wanted to do more. So she opened up a school to teach Black women business skills and help them find employment.

One night, Viola went to the movies. She asked to sit near the screen because it was easier for her to see. But the ticket seller would not sell her a ticket on the main floor. So she bought the balcony ticket he offered her and took a seat in the front of the theater anyway. The manager told her she had to move. The front section, he explained, was for white people only. He said if she didn't move, he would call the police.

Viola refused to move.

Once the police arrived, they grabbed her, dragged her out, and threw her in jail for the night. She was fined for not paying the correct amount of tax for the downstairs ticket (though she had offered to). She tried to sue the theater for discrimination but did not get justice.

Viola's courage was not forgotten. Decades later, the Canadian government pardoned her, and in 2018, it honored Viola for her defiance of racism and her fight for justice by putting her picture on the $10 bill.

JULY 6, 1914–FEBRUARY 7, 1965

WONDAGURL

MUSIC PRODUCER

It's a bird, it's a plane, it's WondaGurl! This superhero story started when a shy girl named Ebony received her first keyboard. She spent hours tapping the keys, learning how to make melodies.

While everyone else was having sleepovers and birthday parties, Ebony made music. She got a drum pad to add rhythmic beats on top of the smooth sound of the keys. She studied the work of famous producers like Timbaland and Hit-Boy. Ebony gave herself a stage name too: WondaGurl— fitting for a girl with musical superpowers.

After a few years of practice, WondaGurl took her music to a beat battle where producers duke it out to see who can make the most creative beats. The first year WondaGurl entered, she didn't perform as well as she hoped. In 2012, she went again.

Onstage under bright purple lights, WondaGurl started playing her tracks. The audience easily found the rhythm and moved to the music. As her beats played, she held her head high, but when the judges were deliberating, nerves took over. Her mom reminded her that if she really wanted this, she needed to face her fears.

She took deep breaths as the judges made the announcement. *And the winner is . . . WondaGurl!* She couldn't stop smiling.

She has produced for Travis Scott, Drake, and Rihanna. She also mentors other young producers. With every success, WondaGurl becomes more and more confident. "The more I grow, and the more I'm in this industry, I feel a lot better and I just feel a lot more comfortable within myself," she says, which of course is another kind of superpower.

BORN DECEMBER 28, 1996

WRITE YOUR STORY

DRAW YOUR PORTRAIT

 # KEEP EXPLORING!

Inventor Andini Makosinski is here to share some fun activities inspired by the Rebels in this book.

CREATE A HOMEMADE CART

When I was a kid, I didn't have all the same toys as my friends, which on occasion made me feel like I was missing out. However, I soon realized that I could *make* my own one-of-a-kind toys at home, using whatever I had around me. This experience led me to grow my imagination and creative, practical skills. Let's give it a try! Today, we'll make a cart.

1. First, gather your materials: a shoebox, a pair of old foam flip-flops, scissors, a pair of chopsticks or a couple of wooden BBQ skewers, and a strong piece of rope or twine.
2. Cut out four big circles of the same size from the flip-flops. These will be your wheels.
3. Now take your scissors and carefully poke a hole in the center of each circle. You can ask an adult to help you with this part.
4. Poke two holes on each of the long sides of the shoebox, about an inch from each bottom corner.
5. Push one stick through the first two holes so it sticks out a little on both ends. The stick should be longer than the width of the box. Repeat with the second set of holes.
6. Stick one of your foam circles on each end of the sticks so you have four wheels.
7. Poke a hole in the center of one end of the box.
8. Pull the rope through the hole and tie a knot to keep it in place. You can now pull your new cart around. Maybe put some of your favorite toys in it!

GROW YOUR OWN GARDEN

Rebels like Autumn Peltier and Angelique Ahlström are working hard to save our environment. Even if you don't have Angelique's special drone to help plant trees, you can still make an impact on your own local greenery. Plant a mini forest garden of your own!

1. Scope out the environment you live in, whether it's an apartment, house, or room. Choose a good space to grow some plants. Make sure you look for a place where your plants will be able to get some sun.
2. Ask your grown-ups for any old containers they have that they aren't using, or ransack your recycling box till you find something that could work. Don't buy a container for your plants—we're trying to be eco-friendly.
3. Fill your containers with dirt. You can find some in your yard or a local park or head to a nursery or garden store with a grown-up.
4. Find some seeds. You can buy a packet or see if any trees or plants in your neighborhood are releasing seeds that you could collect. Dandelions and acorns are usually easy to find!
5. Water your seeds as necessary and watch them grow.

Taking care of a plant is a big responsibility, and it will teach you about showing up and committing to a project: fostering another life on our beautiful planet.

CRAFT A HIT SINGLE

Celine Dion was 12 when she composed her first song, "Nothing but a Dream," with her mother's and brother Jacques' help. Writing a song and then singing it takes a lot of bravery because you have to be vulnerable and share your creation with the audience. Try it out by writing your own song!

1. Think about the things in your life that you love. Do any particular topics, animals, or activities come to mind? Choose one that you think you could have fun writing a song about.
2. Write a few short lines about your chosen topic. This may take some time, but approach it like you're writing a poem.
3. Read the lines out loud to make sure you like the flow.
4. Hum a tune that sounds pleasant to your ear. This can take a few tries—and that's okay! Experimentation and not getting things "perfect" the first few tries are crucial parts of the creative process. Maybe listen to some songs you like for inspiration.
5. Sing your lines according to your chosen tune. Now you have your very own original song!
6. If you feel comfortable, perform your song for someone you feel safe with—a friend, grown-up, or your class! Sharing your art can inspire other people to be brave and creative with their own skills.

FIND A STRONG FEMALE CHARACTER

Anita Sarkeesian noticed the way girls and women were being represented and wanted to change it for the better. Let's think about some of your favorite movies or television shows and what kinds of female characters they have.

1. Get a pen and paper and write down your top 10 movies or television shows of all time.
2. Choose two or three shows or movies from your list that you think you know the most about (or have watched and rewatched the most times!).
3. For each one, write down the names of the main female character(s).
4. Start listing the characters' attributes, qualities, personalities, and styles. Also think about each character's arc—that means a character's own individual storyline within the bigger movie or television show plot. Here are some questions to ask about your character:
    - Do they have their own adventure and life? Or do they come second to a male protagonist?
    - Are they someone you could look up to?
    - Are they complicated? Do they have flaws and strengths just like a real person, or do they feel more superficial?
    - What would happen in the plot if they weren't on the show? Do they save the day, or do they stand more to the side?
5. Make a presentation to your friends or grown-ups about your selected female characters—and add what you would change about them (or perhaps keep the same). Maybe you'll be inspired to write your own short film or story with a female protagonist that resonates with you and who you aspire to be!

LISTEN TO MORE EMPOWERING STORIES ON THE REBEL GIRLS APP!

Download the app to listen to beloved Rebel Girls stories. Filled with the adventures and accomplishments of women from around the world and throughout history, the Rebel Girls app is designed to entertain, inspire, and build confidence in listeners everywhere.

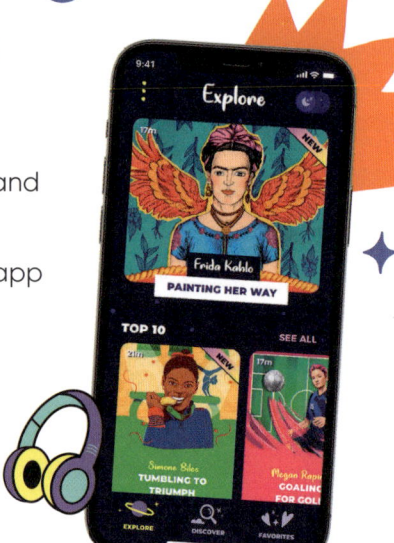

THE ILLUSTRATORS

Twenty-three extraordinary female artists from all over the world illustrated the portraits in this book.

ANDRESSA MEISSNER, **BRAZIL**, 31
ANJA REPONEN, **FINLAND**, 51
AVANI DWIVEDI, **INDIA**, 43
BETSY FALCO, **UK**, 41
CAMILLA RU, **UK**, 55
CHANELLE NIBBELINK, **CANADA**, 25, 33
CHANGYU ZOU, **CHINA**, 37
CLAUDIA CARIERI, **ITALY**, 7
ERICA ROOT, **USA**, 29
EVA RUST, **SWITZERLAND**, 47
JENNY MEILIHOVE, **ISRAEL**, 13
JING LI, **CHINA**, 15

KASIA BOGDAŃSKA, **POLAND**, 35
KATELUN C. BREWSTER, **TRINIDAD AND TOBAGO**, 11
KIMBERLIE CLINTHORNE-WONG, **USA**, 27
LAURA PROIETTI, **ITALY**, 17
LAUWAART, **MARTINIQUE**, 53
MAYA MCKIBBIN, **CANADA**, 19
MICHELLE SIMPSON, **CANADA**, 49
ROXANNE RAINVILLE, **CANADA**, 21
SALINI PERERA, **CANADA**, 9, 23
SASHA KOLESNIK, **RUSSIA**, 45
VIVIENNE SHAO, **UK**, 39

MORE BOOKS!

For more stories about amazing women and girls, check out other Rebel Girls books.

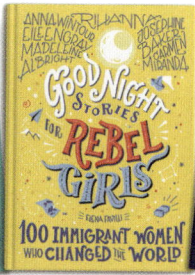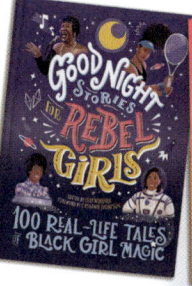

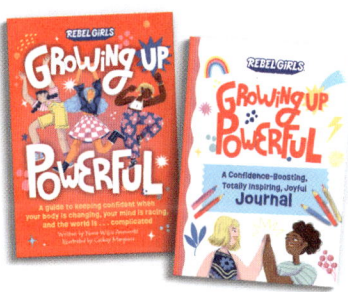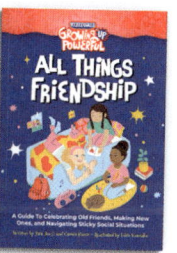

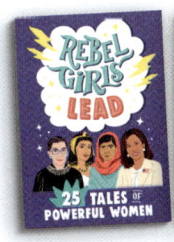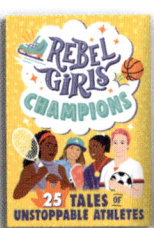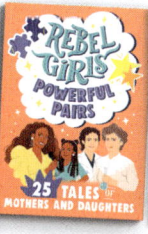

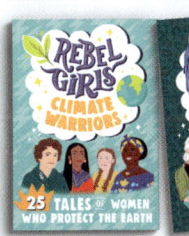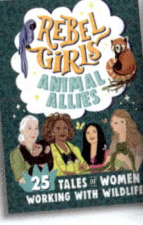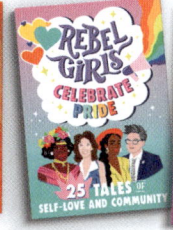

ABOUT REBEL GIRLS

REBEL GIRLS, a certified B Corporation, is a global, multi-platform empowerment brand dedicated to helping raise the most inspired and confident generation of girls through content, experiences, products, and community. Originating from an international best-selling children's book, Rebel Girls amplifies stories of real-life, extraordinary women throughout history, geography, and field of excellence. With a growing community of 30 million self-identified Rebel Girls spanning more than 100 countries, the brand engages with Generation Alpha through its book series, premier app and audio content, events, and merchandise. To date, Rebel Girls has sold more than 11 million books in 50 languages and reached 40 million audio listens. Award recognition includes the *New York Times* bestseller list, the 2022 Apple Design Award for Social Impact, multiple Webby Awards for family & kids and education, and Common Sense Media Selection honors, among many others.

As a B Corp, we're part of a global community of businesses that meet high standards of social and environmental impact.

Join the Rebel Girls community:
  Facebook: facebook.com/rebelgirls
  Instagram: @rebelgirls
  X/Twitter: @rebelgirlsbook
  TikTok: @rebelgirlsbook
  App: rebelgirls.com/audio
  Podcast: rebelgirls.com/podcast
  Web: rebelgirls.com

If you liked this book, please take a moment to review it wherever you prefer!